Essential Events

THE MANHATTAN
PROJECT

Essential Events

THE MANHATTAN
PROJECT

BY SUE VANDER HOOK

Content Consultant
Rebecca Collinsworth, archivist
Los Alamos Historical Museum Archives

ABDO
Publishing Company

CREDITS

Published by ABDO Publishing Company, 8000 West 78th Street, Edina, Minnesota 55439. Copyright © 2011 by Abdo Consulting Group, Inc. International copyrights reserved in all countries. No part of this book may be reproduced in any form without written permission from the publisher. The Essential Library™ is a trademark and logo of ABDO Publishing Company.

Printed in the United States of America,
North Mankato, Minnesota
112010
012011

 THIS BOOK CONTAINS AT LEAST 10% RECYCLED MATERIALS.

Editor: Rebecca Rowell
Copy Editor: Nicholas Cafarelli
Interior Design and Production: Kazuko Collins
Cover Design: Emily Love

Library of Congress Cataloging-in-Publication Data
Vander Hook, Sue, 1949-
   The Manhattan Project / By Sue Vander Hook.
       p. cm. -- (Essential events)
   Includes bibliographical references and index.
   ISBN 978-1-61714-767-8
   1. Manhattan Project (U.S.)--Juvenile literature. 2. Atomic bomb--United States--History--Juvenile literature. I. Title.
   QC773.3.U5V36 2011
   355.8'25119097309044--dc22
                                          2010041429

TABLE OF CONTENTS

*Dorothy Scarritt McKibbin and J. Robert Oppenheimer
first met in Santa Fe, New Mexico.*

GATEKEEPER TO
LOS ALAMOS

Forty-five-year-old Dorothy Scarritt
McKibbin walked confidently into the
elegant lobby of La Fonda Hotel in the heart of
downtown Santa Fe, New Mexico. It was March 26,
1943, and the single mother was about to take a job

she knew nothing about. Nearly everyone in this desert community was familiar to her, but there were new people milling about the town whom she had never seen before.

THE MAN WITH MAGNETISM

McKibbin's old friend Joe Stevenson had stopped the widow in the middle of the street just the day before. Stevenson asked if McKibbin would like to have a job as a secretary. Stevenson could not tell her any details—it was top secret—and he gave her 24 hours to decide.

McKibbin was intrigued by the mystery, so she showed up at La Fonda the next day. Stevenson was there with a man named Duane Muncy, who said he was the manager of a new government housing project. As they talked, a charming man in a trench coat and porkpie hat walked up. Holding his pipe, he said hello to the two men, and they introduced him to McKibbin.

The man left as quickly as he had appeared, and McKibbin did not remember his name. But he had approved of McKibbin and told Stevenson to offer her the job. McKibbin did not hesitate to tell Stevenson she would take it. The vitality and radiance of this fleeting man had grabbed her immediately, and McKibbin knew she wanted to join him in whatever job he was offering. "I never met a person with a magnetism that hit you so fast and so completely as his did," she recalled. "I knew that anything he was connected with would be alive."[1]

Top Secret Mission

The man called himself Mr. Bradley, but he was J. Robert Oppenheimer, a 39-year-old physics professor at the University of California at Berkeley. He was also the newly appointed director of a secret weapons laboratory in Los Alamos, approximately 35 miles (56 km) northwest of Santa Fe. It was part of the Manhattan Project—the code name for a top secret wartime mission.

Oppenheimer had instantly recognized McKibbin's strength and knew she would not easily be unnerved. She started work the next day. Her office was in an inconspicuous, unmarked downtown Santa Fe building at 109 East Palace Avenue. Every day, McKibbin answered hundreds of telephone calls and issued passes, mostly to scientists and their families. Everyone needed a pass to get into the compound, which was called the Hill. It was located on top of a desert mesa at the end of a steep, twisting mountain road. When the weather was bad, it could take as long as four hours to get there from Santa Fe.

TRUSTED GATEKEEPER

"Dink," as Oppenheimer came to call McKibbin, became known as the gatekeeper to Los Alamos. No one got to the Hill without first going through McKibbin. She approved the highest security passes—the Q badges—for some of the most brilliant, Nobel Prize-winning physicists

109 East Palace Avenue

The Santa Fe, New Mexico, office of the Manhattan Project closed on June 28, 1963. A brief ceremony memorialized the site and marked McKibbin's retirement after 20 years. Norris Bradbury, a physicist who had helped construct the atomic bomb, thanked the woman who was 109 East Palace Avenue. He presented the mayor of Santa Fe with a bronze plaque that hangs at the site.

1943　　　SANTA FE OFFICE　　　1963
LOS ALAMOS SCIENTIFIC LABORATORY
UNIVERSITY OF CALIFORNIA

All the men and women who made the first atomic bomb passed through this portal to the secret mission at Los Alamos. Their creation in 27 months of the weapons that ended World War II was one of the greatest scientific achievements of all time.[2]

In 1979, the College of Santa Fe awarded McKibbin an honorary degree that read,

Out of the 1940s came developments in scientific research which changed the course of world history. . . . In the very midst of this tense, top-secret, wartime pandemonium stood a calm, intelligent, efficient and loving woman: Dorothy Scarritt McKibbin.[3]

McKibbin died on December 17, 1985. She was 88.

and chemists in the world. She made arrangements for their families, their luggage, their household possessions, and anything they needed to get settled.

When the laboratory on the Hill opened, Oppenheimer and 30 other scientists took up residence there with their families. For at least 12 hours a day, the researchers scrawled mathematical calculations on blackboards and napkins, and they discussed how their formulas might work. In the evening, the scientists and their families usually ate at Fuller Lodge. There, they would sometimes bring out their musical instruments and perform concerts together or square-dance the night away to do-si-do music.

The Hill also swarmed with metallurgists and explosives experts. There were nonscientists as well, who were contracted for construction work. They erected laboratory buildings and apartments. Military personnel ran the base. They guarded this covert compound that was fenced in with steel wire and surrounded with mystery. They especially

By 1950, Los Alamos looked very different than it had during the Manhattan Project.

safeguarded the Tech Area—known simply as the "T"—an interior area enclosed with a 9.5-foot (3-m) fence with two strands of barbed wire on top.

TRINITY

The project would culminate in July 1945, more than two years after McKibbin started her secretarial job. It was an extraordinarily hot summer in New Mexico that year. Scientists were putting in long hours at the compound, especially inside the T. Traffic increased on the road south of Los Alamos. People and equipment were on their way to a place

LANL

The Los Alamos National Laboratory, where the first atomic bomb was built, is still in operation today. More than 1,300 buildings cover this more than 40-square-mile (103-sq-km) spread of laboratories and testing facilities. Most of its 9,000 employees and 650 contractors are physicists, engineers, and chemists.

called Jornada del Muerto, which is Spanish for "Journey of Death." Sporadic explosions were going off. Oppenheimer told his workers that the target date for Trinity—the code name for the test of their work—was Monday, July 16.

On July 15, Oppenheimer gazed one last time at the device he called "the gadget"—a large, crude sphere covered with precisely placed plugs and a chaotic entanglement of wires. Then, Oppenheimer joined some of the scientists who had worked on his project. All of them paced the floor throughout the night, unable to sleep, peering out into the dark, stormy sky.

McKibbin was in a car that night, gazing to the south and waiting with a friend on the peak of Sandia Mountain in Albuquerque, New Mexico. It was raining and dark. She knew something breathtaking was about to happen, but there was no way she could have imagined the mind-boggling explosion that was about to take place. She had no idea how huge it would be, or how it would forever change the world. The atomic bomb had been created.

*Oppenheimer led scientific research in Los Alamos
that forever changed the world.*

The US government's Manhattan Project began as New York City's Manhattan Engineer District.

THE MANHATTAN PROJECT

The Manhattan Project began in the summer of 1942 in New York City, on the island of Manhattan. It was in a section designated the Manhattan Engineer District, the army's headquarters for a new project—the development of an atomic weapon. Although a project of the US Army, not all of the scientists who worked on it were American.

GERMANY'S SCIENTISTS

When the Manhattan Project began, World War II had been raging in Europe for three years, and Adolf Hitler had been in power in Germany for more than nine. During that time, Hitler passed laws that methodically shut down Jewish businesses and discriminated against anyone who was not Aryan. He believed that only blond-haired, blue-eyed Nordics were worthy of citizenship. Non-Aryans, mostly Jews, left the country in droves for fear of their lives and in search of work elsewhere.

Germany lost thousands of Jewish business owners, university professors, and scientists, including about one-fourth of the country's physicists. Many of Germany's most brilliant citizens escaped Hitler's race laws and fled to other countries, including Sweden, Denmark, and the United States.

Exiled Scientists

Adolf Hitler forced more than 60 percent of Jews to leave Germany. Some of the German Jews who sought exile abroad in the 1930s and 1940s were the world's greatest scientists. Albert Einstein, Edward Teller, Otto Frisch, Lise Meitner, Leo Szilard, and others who had already made giant strides in atomic research left their homeland to avoid persecution by the Nazis.

Some of the exiled scientists knew about important scientific research going on in Germany. At the Kaiser Wilhelm Institute of Chemistry in Berlin, Germany's capital, physicists and chemists were experimenting with the nucleus of an atom. They wanted to find out what would happen if the nucleus split into smaller nuclei and wondered if some sort of energy would be released. In late 1938, German chemists Otto Hahn and Fritz Strassmann bombarded a uranium atom with neutrons.

The Mighty Atom

All matter is made up of atoms. These tiny particles pack a massive amount of energy. More than 2,400 years ago, Greek philosopher Democritus called them *atomos*, a Greek word meaning "not cuttable." Later, scientists discovered that an atom has three types of particles: protons, neutrons, and electrons. The center, or nucleus, has protons and neutrons. Electrons zip around the nucleus.

The uranium-235 atom is an isotope: it has an unequal number of protons and neutrons. It is considered unstable—radioactive. Isotopes are constantly changing and firing electrons and particles from the nucleus. In 1934, Italian physicist Enrico Fermi figured out how to use these active particles to bombard other atoms. German scientists took Fermi's work further. A few years later, they fired neutrons at a uranium atom and witnessed an amazing change. Uranium turned into a completely different element. One year later, scientists discovered that the atom could split and release large amounts of energy.

The next step was realizing that splitting atoms could lead to a chain reaction. When neutrons split an atom, energy and more neutrons were released. These neutrons then shot out at a high speed and split more atoms, releasing yet more neutrons and energy, and so forth. Thus began a nuclear chain reaction and the idea for an atomic bomb.

The nucleus split—nuclear fission had occurred. According to the scientists, the result was astounding.

The Einstein Letter

It was 1939 before the United States became aware of Germany's experiment with nuclear fission. In July, Hungarian scientists Leo Szilard and Eugene Wigner met with German physicist Albert Einstein. They convened in Long Island, New York, where Einstein was spending the summer. The men discussed how nuclear fission made it possible to construct a bomb and how to keep more of the world's uranium from falling into Nazi hands. Einstein agreed to write a warning letter to the US ambassador to the Belgian Congo, a country with a large stockpile of uranium.

Within a few days, Alexander Sachs, economic adviser to US President Franklin D. Roosevelt, urged Einstein to write a letter to the president. Roosevelt had to be warned that Germany may already have

Albert Einstein

Albert Einstein was no longer living in Germany when Adolf Hitler came to power there in 1933. Einstein had left his homeland in 1932 and later renounced his German citizenship. He toured Europe giving speeches about Nazi Germany. Einstein and his wife settled in Princeton, New Jersey, where he became a professor of theoretical physics at the Institute for Advanced Study.

been making an atomic weapon. Einstein dictated a two-page letter in German that Szilard translated into English. The letter, dated August 2, 1939, told the president:

> The element uranium may be turned into a new and important source of energy in the immediate future. . . . It may become possible to set up a nuclear chain reaction in a large mass of uranium, by which vast amounts of power and large quantities of new radiumlike elements would be generated. . . . This new phenomenon would also lead to the construction of bombs, and it is conceivable—though much less certain—that extremely powerful bombs of a new type may thus be constructed.[1]

Einstein's letter did not reach Roosevelt until October 11. In the meantime, Germany invaded Poland on September 1. Then, Great Britain and France declared war on Germany. World War II had begun. Roosevelt eventually responded to Einstein's letter:

> My dear Professor:
>
> I want to thank you for your recent letter and the most interesting and important enclosure.

Albert Einstein and other European scientists worried about Nazi Germany.

I found this data of such import that I have convened a Board consisting of the head of the Bureau of Standards and a chosen representative of the Army and Navy to thoroughly investigate the possibilities of your suggestion regarding the element of uranium.

I am glad to say that Dr. Sachs will cooperate and work with this Committee and I feel this is the most practical and effective method of dealing with the subject.

Please accept my sincere thanks.

Very sincerely yours,

(signed) Franklin D. Roosevelt[2]

Roosevelt organized a board to investigate uranium and nuclear fission. The president approved the secret formation of the Advisory Committee on Uranium with a budget of $6,000. The first meeting was held in Washington DC on October 21, 1939. Scientists began looking for sources of uranium and experimenting with how to form it into a weapon. They tested nuclear fission— the splitting of atoms—and how chain reactions could produce an explosion.

The MAUD Committee

In England, a top secret group was also formed. MAUD met for the first time on April 10, 1940. Meanwhile, news came from Eugene Wigner, a reliable source: "German physicists are working intensively on the problem of the uranium bomb."[3]

Word was out that Germany had an ample supply of uranium. The race was on to produce an atomic bomb before Germany did.

American engineer Vannevar Bush urged Roosevelt to establish an agency for research into nuclear energy. Roosevelt agreed and put Bush in charge of what was called the National Defense Research Committee. Its purpose was to "support scientific research on the mechanisms and devices of warfare."[4] A year later, it would become part of the Office of Scientific Research and Development, the government agency that would one day control the Manhattan Project.

In July 1941, the British ended their research. MAUD Committee members wrote their report and parted ways. The committee's final report concluded that a bomb could be made from what was called uranium-235. It would require 25 pounds (11 kg) of uranium, and the resulting explosion would equal 1,800 tons (1,633 metric tons) of TNT. It was enough explosive power to wipe out an entire city.

TNT

TNT is trinitrotoluene, a yellowish chemical compound used as explosive material. The explosive power of TNT is the standard measurement for energy released by bombs. Since nuclear explosions are so massive, their explosive energy is measured in tons, kilotons, or megatons of TNT power. Scientists also measure the impact of colliding comets or meteoroids by TNT power.

Great Britain admitted it did not have the resources
to conduct the project and gave the report to the
United States.

Attack on Pearl Harbor

On December 6, 1941, the United States began
a program of accelerated research in atomic energy.
The next morning, on December 7, the Japanese
Empire attacked Pearl Harbor in Hawaii. Air-raid
sirens screamed as wave after wave of Japanese planes
dropped bombs on US battleships and airfields.
For nearly an hour, Japan waged its massive surprise
attack on the United States. Four battleships sank,
two of which were destroyed. There were 188 US
planes completely destroyed and 159 damaged—most
while still parked on the tarmac. The wounded
numbered 1,178, and the death toll was 2,403.
Never before had so many Americans lost their lives
in one attack.

The next day, December 8, the United States
declared war on Japan. Three days later, Germany
and Italy declared war on the United States. After
avoiding entering the war for several years, the
United States was thrust into the ongoing world
conflict of World War II.

The Japanese attack on Pearl Harbor on December 7, 1941, finally drew the United States into World War II after taking a passive role in the war for more than two years.

Japan's air attacks extended beyond Pearl Harbor to several island nations in the Pacific Ocean. Japanese forces swept through Indonesia, Malaya, Guam, the Philippines, Wake Island, and Midway Island. And Germany continued its expansion, crushing European nations in its path.

US scientists were keeping a watchful eye on their German counterparts when it came to nuclear research. In May 1942, James B. Conant, president

of Harvard University and president
of the National Defense Research
Committee, reported, "There are
still plenty of competent scientists
left in Germany. They may be ahead
of us by as much as a year, but hardly
more."[5]

Conducting nuclear research and
experiments became increasingly
important. In August 1942, eight
months after entering the war, the
United States created the Manhattan
Project. US Army General Leslie
Groves was put in charge of the
project, including the first secret site,
located in Manhattan. Four more
top secret sites would be established:
Oak Ridge, Tennessee; Los Alamos,
New Mexico; Hanford, Washington;
and Wendover, Utah.

"The unleashed power of the atom has changed everything save our modes of thinking and we thus drift toward unparalleled catastrophe."[6]

—*Albert Einstein in a telegram to prominent Americans quoted in* New York Times *magazine, 25 May 1946*

Leslie Groves

Workers at Site X in Oak Ridge, Tennessee

Sites X and Y

In September 1942, Groves purchased 59,000 acres (23,876 ha) on behalf of the United States. The land was in the remote hill country of Oak Ridge, Tennessee—a huge area simply dubbed "Site X." There, well hidden from curious eyes, the US Army built factories and laboratories to study uranium. Scientists researched different types of uranium isotopes. They found uranium-235 (U-235) the best isotope for a nuclear chain reaction. But nature provided very little U-235, so Site X would concentrate on producing the substance.

Army engineers worked throughout the winter and spring of 1942–1943 to produce what looked like an entire town in an unlikely area of Tennessee. Railroads, paved roads, houses, and laboratories were built. The most attention was given to the massive plant where uranium would be enriched—altered to make it usable for nuclear fission. Fences and secured gates restricted the town from anyone who was not part of the Manhattan Project.

Chicago Pile-1

Work on nuclear fission was also moving along quickly throughout the rest of the country. While Site X was being erected, physicist Enrico Fermi was conducting experiments at the

"All scientists at Los Alamos knew that the fission of the atom had been first achieved in Germany. Until after the war, they believed that the Germans were ahead of us in the potentiality of building a bomb, and unless we could be first to achieve it, the United States would be the next nation [conquered]."[1]

—*Dorothy Scarritt McKibbin*

University of Chicago in Illinois. On December 2, 1942, he was on a seldom-used squash court beneath a grandstand at Stagg Field, the university's football stadium. In that unlikely place, he and fellow scientists achieved a nuclear chain reaction. It was called Chicago Pile-1, and it is probably the single most important event in the development of the atomic bomb.

Chicago Pile-1 had been a risky experiment in one of the most crowded cities in the country. It was a 500-ton (454-metric ton) pile of graphite bricks stacked in 57 layers that rose 20 feet (6 m). It took two weeks to build the pile. Cubes of uranium were amid the bricks. Long rods were placed into the bricks—control rods to divert and absorb neutron activity and manage the blast.

On a platform above the pile stood three young men—the "suicide squad"—who would drench the pile with a solution of cadmium salt if the chain reaction got out of control. Physicist George Weil stood next to the pile, slowly pulling rods out to allow the chain reaction to begin. If the experiment went dreadfully wrong, a scientist poised above and armed with an ax was ready to chop through a rope that held a rod designed to stop the reaction.

1/8 SCALE FERMI REACTOR MODEL

A model of Chicago Pile-1, the nuclear test built in a squash court at the University of Chicago. It was a pile of graphite blocks containing lumps of uranium, in a wooden framework.

After more than five hours of experimentation, neutron activity had increased to a rapid intensity. Fermi put his hand in the air and announced, "The pile has gone critical."[2] A few minutes later, he told someone to reinsert the control rod. Fermi smiled. The nuclear chain reaction had been a success.

If Fermi's experiment had failed, the blast would have probably destroyed a large portion of Chicago. Fermi's work showed what a chain reaction could do—release enough energy to create a massive explosion. It also confirmed that atomic power could be controlled.

Arthur Holly Compton, one of the physicists at the stadium, immediately called James B. Conant, head of the National Defense Research Committee. The men spoke in code. Compton said, "The Italian navigator has landed in the New World." Conant asked, "How were the natives?" Compton replied, "Very friendly."[3] Hungarian physicist Leo Szilard was also there, but he viewed the event differently. Szilard shook Fermi's hand and said he thought the day would go down as a "black day in the history of mankind."[4]

GROVES AND OPPIE

Meanwhile, the Manhattan Project continued to progress. Two months before Fermi's Chicago experiment, Groves had appointed physicist J. Robert Oppenheimer as scientific head of the project. Groves and Oppenheimer—or "Oppie" as he was called—were complete opposites in their backgrounds, appearance, habits, interests, religious beliefs, and political ideals. The men were an unlikely pair to run such a critical operation.

But the men's differences did not make it impossible for them to work together. Groves believed Oppenheimer was the right man for this job, and he did not hesitate to appoint Oppenheimer. As different as these two men were, they had high respect for one another and would work well together.

Site Y

Oppenheimer wasted no time organizing the scientific part of the Manhattan Project. The first thing he wanted was a central location where scientists could come together to work. They could brainstorm, design formulas, and eventually create and test a bomb. Oppenheimer got

Opposites

Groves and Oppenheimer were different in every way. Groves was a lifetime military man, stern, tall, and stocky at more than 250 pounds (113 kg). Oppenheimer was a deep thinker and scientist who went from university to university studying and experimenting. Oppenheimer was tall as well, but he was extremely thin at about 130 pounds (59 kg). Groves neither smoked nor drank. Oppie did both daily. Groves was a sports fanatic, especially concerning baseball, while Oppie knew nothing about sports.

Groves and Oppenheimer were also at opposite ends of the religious spectrum. Groves was a devout Christian, the son of a Presbyterian army chaplain. Oppenheimer, raised in a Jewish family who did not practice Judaism, immersed himself in Hindu sacred texts such as the Bhagavad Gita. He knew Sanskrit and could read the Hindu scripture in its original language.

Their politics were also dissimilar. Groves was US Army to the core, conservative and dedicated to democracy. Oppenheimer was far left wing. He was not a communist, but family members and some close friends were members of the Communist Party. Oppenheimer was deeply concerned about the rising prejudice against Jews in Germany and welcomed a way to end the fanatical anti-Semitism that was taking place there.

Los Alamos Ranch School

Los Alamos Ranch School was founded in 1917. It consisted of a few ranch buildings and the Big House, a two-story log building with classrooms, a dining hall, and offices. Students were boys ages 12 to 18. As a college preparatory school, Los Alamos Ranch School had high academic standards. It was unique in its affiliation with the Boy Scouts of America. Students were members of Los Alamos Troop 22. In its 25-year existence, more than 600 boys attended the school.

his request: Site Y at Los Alamos, New Mexico. He had lived in the state for a while, though in a different area. The Oppenheimer family had a cabin in Pecos, which is in the Sangre de Christo Mountains.

Health problems had brought him to this dry land that provided just the right climate for people suffering from many ailments. He had become enchanted with the area and remembered a beautiful plateau where he had once ridden on horseback.

Groves was pleased that many of the Manhattan Project scientists would be in one location. Fences and barbed wire would protect them and maintain higher security for their sensitive research. Groves agreed that New Mexico was an ideal place for the Manhattan Project. It was a good distance from the West Coast, where the Japanese could easily attack. Railways provided connections from nearby Albuquerque to Chicago, Los Angeles, San Francisco, and Washington DC. And all TWA coast-to-coast flights stopped in Albuquerque to refuel.

Los Alamos Ranch School

The only activity then on the large mesa that was chosen to be Site Y was the Los Alamos Ranch School. Boys ages 12 to 18 lived a rigorous and healthy outdoor life there while receiving a first-rate college preparatory education. Each boy was assigned a horse, participated in sports and camping, did service projects, and attended classes. But the Manhattan Project wanted the land. The school would have to go, and the US Army took over neighboring homestead properties.

On December 7, 1942, exactly one year after the Japanese attacked Pearl Harbor, Hawaii, the school director read a letter to the students and faculty. It was from US Secretary of War Henry L. Stimson. The letter stated that the army was taking over the school's property in "the interests of the United States in the prosecution of the War."[5]

School officials asked to stay there until the end of the school year, but their request was denied. The school cancelled its Christmas holidays and accelerated the school schedule so the boys could complete their school year early. On January 21, 1943, the last of the students received their diplomas. Outside, bulldozers were already digging up the volcanic rock to prepare for what would eventually house a main building, five laboratories, a warehouse, a machine shop, barracks, and basic apartments. Every day, huge military trucks climbed the steep pass to Los Alamos and rumbled across the plateau. In the end, Site Y would be a large community with a ramshackle mixture of prefabricated buildings. The buildings were brought primarily from other military bases to address the ongoing housing crisis as the number of people at Site Y expanded.

The development looked like a military post, which it was. The buildings, including the military barracks, were built following standard patterns used by military engineers in numerous locations other than Los Alamos.

THE WORLD'S BEST SCIENTISTS

Oppenheimer was pleased with the site and did not hesitate in recruiting the most brilliant scientists in the world to work on the project. He somehow convinced them to pack up their families and "work for a purpose he could not disclose, at a place he could not specify, for a period he could not predict."[6] Hundreds of bright scientists from all over the world came, including Enrico Fermi, Bruno Rossi, Emilio Segrè, Hans Bethe, Edward Teller, and Otto Frisch. Other scientists, such as Niels Bohr and I. I. Rabi, acted as consultants. They did not move to Los Alamos, but they visited and contributed to the research there. Day after day in the spring of 1943, they converged on Santa Fe, where they waited for instructions on how to get to Site Y. One of the physicists was Austrian Victor Weisskopf, who explained his willingness to join Oppenheimer's team:

> I joined enthusiastically because of many reasons. First, my friends and I were very much afraid that the Germans would get it [the atomic bomb] before the United States. Second . . . how could a young man of thirty-five years not join a project of this kind that was full of the best and greatest physicists?[7]

Treacherous Road

The road leading to Los Alamos was treacherous. The Otowi Bridge that spanned the Rio Grande River was narrow and too weak to handle heavy traffic and large military equipment. As a result, traffic was detoured through Española, which added ten miles (16 km) to the already difficult trip.

Nobel Laureates

In 1927, Arthur Holly Compton was awarded the Nobel Prize for Physics with fellow physicist C. T. R. Wilson. The scientists' discovery of how X-rays change—energy from a photon is transferred to an electron—is known as the Compton effect.

Enrico Fermi was awarded the Nobel Prize for Physics in 1938 "for his demonstrations of the existence of new radioactive elements produced by neutron irradiation, and for his related discovery of nuclear reactions brought about by slow neutrons."[10]

Oppenheimer later recalled, "The notion of disappearing into the desert for an indeterminate period and under quasi-military auspices disturbed a good many scientists and the families of many more."[8] The wife of one of the first scientists to be recruited wrote, "I felt akin to the pioneer women accompanying their husbands across uncharted plains westward, alert to dangers, resigned to the fact that they journeyed, for weal or woe, into the Unknown."[9]

*Fermi's work in physics garnered a Nobel Prize in 1938
and led to the development of the Manhattan Project.*

Scientists spent their time at Los Alamos doing things other than research. Some enjoyed playing instruments, such as the piano.

LIFE ON THE HILL

*I*n addition to hiring scientists, Oppenheimer hired administrative personnel to work on the Manhattan Project. One nonscientist was Dorothy Scarritt McKibbin, a widow and mother. Oppenheimer met McKibbin in March 1943, in the lobby of La Fonda Hotel in Santa Fe, New Mexico. He approved her to be the gatekeeper and chief guardian of Site Y, which was also known as the Hill. Her unmarked office was at 109 East Palace Avenue, Santa Fe. Every new arrival—approximately 65 a day at first—stopped at McKibbin's office and received a warm welcome. She calmed their fears and made arrangements for their belongings to be taken to the Hill. McKibbin wrote of the project scientists she met,

> They arrived, those [souls] in transit, breathless, sleepless, haggard and tired. Most of the new arrivals were tense with expectancy and curiosity. They had . . . deceived their friends and launched forth to an unpredictable world.[1]

Moving In

McKibbin also gave the new arrivals information and instructions to the Hill, including a yellow map with 45 miles (72 km) of winding dirt roads, paths, bridges, and turns marked with red pencil. The travelers found a military base where all the buildings except for those of the former Ranch School were clad in the US Army's trademark green.

The Rumor Mill

Los Alamos was the war's best-kept secret. However, rumors ran rampant in Santa Fe. Some thought the Hill was producing poisonous gas. Others called it a concentration camp or hospital, probably because there were so many "doctors" there. Oppenheimer purposely spread the rumor that an electric rocket was being built, a story that stuck for quite a while.

Rising into the clear sky was a cluster of metal chimneys that belched out smoke from the coal, wood, and oil-burning stoves and furnaces that provided heat for cooking and warmth. Buildings from the school were scarcely noticeable among the barracks-looking structures. Spring was muddy, summer was dusty, and winter brought snow.

Residents of Santa Fe could not help but notice the overwhelming presence of the army and hundreds of strangers passing through their city. But most likely, many of them did not ask questions. They knew all too well that the United States was at war and that everyone in the country was doing their part in the war effort.

OTHER PROJECT SITES

While Site X and Site Y were being erected, 45,000 construction workers converged on Hanford, Washington. It was Site W. There, several nuclear reactors were being built for the production of a radioactive element called plutonium. It could be artificially produced by bombarding uranium atoms and releasing neutrons. Eventually, the plutonium would be shipped to the Los Alamos site. Hanford was located in a remote area along the Columbia River, which made it an ideal site. A reactor needed a water source and a power source. Hanford had both. The government took over the area in March 1943, relocating some 1,500 residents of Hanford, White Bluff, and nearby Native American settlements.

In Wendover, Utah, another top secret site was working on ways to transport and deliver large bombs. As part of Project Alberta, more than a few dozen scientists, engineers, and military personnel at Wendover Field created casings for bombs, prepared airplanes to transport them, and devised ways to protect the aircrew from the blast. They came up with the best way to assemble and load nuclear weapons and supervise them during missions. Crews were trained for deployment, and flight tests were conducted. Workers also developed

Environmental Cleanup

Today, the location of the Hanford Site in Washington is the most contaminated nuclear site in the United States. After the plant was shut down in 1989, it left behind 53 million gallons (200,626,825 L) of high-level radioactive waste. The area is the focus of the nation's largest environmental cleanup project.

Several secret facilities across the United States contributed to the Manhattan Project.

protective devices to keep bombs from exploding prematurely on the airplane.

Busy on the Hill

The busiest of the four secret sites was Los Alamos. The Hill opened officially on April 15, 1943. It was a unique community—isolated, secret, and bustling with approximately 1,500 people by the end of its first month of operation. By 1945, there would be more than 6,000 residents on the desert plateau. The community had no paved roads, no street names, and no sidewalks. Housing consisted of makeshift apartment buildings, duplexes, prefabricated houses, and the old school building. A wooden water tower was the only source of water, and, initially, there was only one telephone line.

Because some Los Alamos personnel had children, a school was established in 1943. It had 12 grades and 16 teachers. The site did not have a dentist until 1944. That same year, Los Alamos got a hospital. Los Alamos also had a town council, elected by the people, to decide community matters. Eventually, laundry and dry cleaning services began, along with a nursery school and a maid service that employed Native American women from a nearby pueblo.

The site had theater productions, orchestra performances, and movies. In the midst of isolation and hardship, the residents developed a social and cultural atmosphere on an isolated desert mesa. A single mission united them: win the war.

Armed military personnel constantly guarded the compound.

Music on the Hill

Music was an important part of the Los Alamos community. A radio station on the Hill staffed by the military, including the announcers, provided a wide variety of music. Chamber orchestras met regularly for practice and performance. Two singing groups, one small and one large, offered annual performances of Handel's *Messiah*. Dancing became the rage, especially square dances, polkas, and waltzes.

They patrolled the perimeter of the fence and watched the surrounding canyons and mountains. It was difficult for some of the scientists and their wives and children to get used to such tight security. They could not venture more than 100 miles (161 km) from the compound, and they were allowed to visit Santa Fe only once a month. The presence of too many unknown faces at once, or faces of famous scientists that might be recognized, was not a good idea. Workers at Site Y could never have contact with relatives or friends. They looked forward to rare shopping days and luncheons, usually

A Little Eccentric

George Marchi was the chef at Los Alamos. According to Marchi, some of the scientists who worked on the Manhattan Project were rather quirky. For example, physicist Edward Teller often played the piano—even in the middle of the night. And another scientist was fined for leaving out top secret information overnight, but he refused to pay. The scientist explained that the top secret information, which was written by a colleague, was completely incorrect and that leaving it out where an enemy spy could steal it was a good thing.

Another oddity became apparent when scientists got sick. Rather than go to the clinic, they went to the library to look up their own symptoms and diagnose their own illnesses. In spite of personalities that were a bit odd, the Los Alamos scientists worked together with surprising unity. Kathleen Mark, wife of Canadian mathematician J. Carson Mark, said, "But when one considers that we lived, day after day, year after year, closely packed together . . . one can't help but marvel that we enjoyed each other so much."[2]

at La Fonda. But that could also be a distressing experience. One resident of Los Alamos recalled, "I couldn't go to Santa Fe without being aware of hidden eyes upon me, watching, waiting to pounce on that inevitable misstep. It wasn't a pleasant feeling."[3]

HIDDEN IDENTITIES

The names of some of the most famous scientists were changed while they were at Los Alamos. Enrico Fermi was "Henry Farmer." Niels Bohr, Nobel laureate for his work in atomic structure and quantum physics, was called "Nicholas Baker" or "Uncle Nick." And the word *physicist* was banned. Everyone was an engineer. Scientists with PhDs were no longer called by the title of doctor—just mister. Names on driver's licenses, car titles, bank accounts, tax returns, and insurance policies were changed to numbers. Children born at Los Alamos were given a Santa Fe post office box as an address. All incoming mail to the Hill was simply addressed P.O. Box 1663, Santa Fe, New Mexico. The government did not want to draw anyone's attention to Los Alamos.

The brightest minds in the world were living restricted lives and given countless rules to follow under less-than-adequate living conditions. They were not allowed to tell their spouses about the work they were doing. Researchers worked a minimum of 48 hours a week, often into the evenings. When a need for secretaries, teachers, technicians, draftspersons, or librarians arose, the scientists' wives sometimes stepped forward. They had not planned to work at the site, but when they were needed, they helped. In their spare time, usually on Sundays, many Los Alamos residents packed picnic lunches and went to Bandelier National Monument several miles away. The view there was breathtaking. They hiked, explored the canyon, and went horseback riding. In the winter, they donned their skis or ice skates and took part in winter sports.

"Almost everyone knew that this job, if it were achieved, would be part of history. This sense of excitement, of devotion and of patriotism in the end prevailed."[5]

—J. Robert Oppenheimer

The people of the Hill stayed in the secluded, guarded location and got along rather well. General Groves admitted that it was not easy keeping everyone happy and meeting their demands. He once called them "the largest collection of crackpots ever seen."[4] But they were getting the job done, they were united, and Groves and Oppenheimer were pleased.

*Scientist Niels Bohr took advantage of New Mexico's
winter snow and enjoyed skiing.*

Oppenheimer, right, meets with one of his researchers.

Two Weapons

The job ahead of Oppenheimer and the other scientists was enormous, and it would be a long road to turn Fermi's Chicago Pile-1 into a weapon of mass destruction. The theory of the weapon had been proven, but now it was time to actually make the weapon. One of the first things Oppenheimer did at Los Alamos was ban the word *bomb*. The weapon would be called "gadget" instead.

In fall 1943, President Franklin D. Roosevelt and British Prime Minister Winston Churchill met to discuss the war. Churchill agreed to send several of Britain's top scientists to Los Alamos. They joined the other scientists who were experimenting with splitting uranium atoms. The scientists at Los Alamos used particle accelerators—commonly called atom smashers—to bombard uranium with neutrons. The researchers tested with both fast-moving and slow-moving neutrons. Their experiments found that a good quality bomb dropped from the air needed millions of fast neutrons. And the scientists developed initiators, devices that produced millions of neutrons.

THIN MAN

Los Alamos scientists also had to figure out how to make the bomb go off at just the right time. A nuclear bomb does not have a fuse that

Borrowed Equipment

The Los Alamos site used several pieces of borrowed equipment. A cyclotron (particle accelerator) was on loan from Harvard University. The University of Wisconsin provided temporary use of two electrostatic accelerators, and the University of Illinois shared a Cockcroft-Walton accelerator.

someone lights and waits for the explosion. Once the chain reaction starts, there is no stopping it.

The first nuclear bomb constructed at Los Alamos was "Thin Man." It was a long, gun-type weapon. Research involved using both uranium and plutonium. In 1944, scientists working on the bomb realized the gun was impractical and would most likely explode unexpectedly. Nuclear fission was too powerful for such a small weapon, and premature detonation was the problem. Scientists abandoned Thin Man to focus on a weapon with a different method.

Scientist Seth H. Neddermeyer suggested a new idea for a bomb. It came to be known as the theory of implosion. Implosion begins with a mass of uranium or plutonium that is compressed violently by high explosives that go off around it. When compressed enough, the material reaches a supercritical state. Next, atoms split one after another in a chain reaction. The idea was completely new. At first, some were skeptical. But since it would require less of the precious uranium or plutonium, research went forward.

THE GADGET: THE FIRST ATOMIC BOMB

Throughout 1943 and 1944, workers at Site X, Site Y, Site W, Wendover Field, and universities across the United States focused on one thing: the gadget. Work was slow with frustrating experiments into the unknown realm of nuclear science. But there was one thing for sure: the gadget had to be tested before it was dropped over enemy territory. No one knew how big the explosion

Teller's Ultimate Catastrophe

When the Thin Man did not work as scientists had hoped, physicists on the project suggested alternatives. Edward Teller proposed that the heat inside an exploding bomb could be used to ignite hydrogen. However, Teller admitted that his calculations showed the explosion could possibly set the atmosphere and the oceans on fire. It might destroy Earth as they knew it. Oppenheimer was troubled by Teller's findings and consulted with physicist Arthur Compton, who called it "the ultimate catastrophe." Compton said it was "better to accept the slavery of the Nazis than run a chance of drawing a final curtain on mankind!"[1]

In the end, Teller's calculations about a hydrogen bomb contained some errors. There was only about one chance in 3 million that the bomb would set the atmosphere on fire. But that did not calm the fears of many of the scientists at Los Alamos. They wondered if what they were doing could ultimately wreak havoc on the entire planet. It was important to them to change the course of history by winning the most dangerous war the world had ever seen, but they certainly did not want to bring on worldwide disaster.

would be. The scientists wanted to know how much radiation would be released and what the radioactive fallout would be. The researchers did not know if there would be a fireball or a smoke cloud. Only a test run would tell.

Meanwhile, the war in Europe was beginning to turn against Hitler and his Nazis. Germany was forced to withdraw from areas such as North Africa and Italy. The Allies were seizing the offensive and pummeling German cities with thousands of tons of traditional bombs in relentless air raids.

In spring 1944, physicists, chemists, engineers, and explosives experts moved closer to a test-ready gadget. More and more people were coming to Los Alamos to work on the project. Conditions were crowded in the ramshackle city, tensions were high, and there was an incredible urgency to finish the bomb.

Harvard chemist George Kistiakowsky was the leading explosives expert in the United States. He moved to the Hill and brought detonation experts and more explosives specialists, including Harvard physicist Kenneth Bainbridge. Small samples of plutonium were arriving from Hanford and Oak Ridge. Rudimentary computers arrived for the first

Men and women worked on the Manhattan Project.

time and immediately began calculating implosion formulas faster than physicists could do by hand. Scientists needed the best answers in the least amount of time.

The unique transportation container for the gadget was also taking shape. "Jumbo" was the code name for the steel container that would house the bomb. In the end, it would be 25 feet (7.6 m) long, 12 feet (3.7 m) in diameter with walls 14 inches (36 cm) thick. It would weigh 214 tons (194 metric tons).

Baby Boom

While atoms were being split
and the gadget was being built, a
baby boom was taking place at Los
Alamos. Eighty babies had been
born in 1943—an average of about
seven babies per month. The average
increased in 1944. Records for
June showed that approximately
one-fifth of the married women
were pregnant, including Kitty
Oppenheimer. One-sixth of the Los
Alamos population was children.
Apartments were becoming crowded,
washing machines were breaking
down, power generators were
sometimes unreliable, and gasoline
sometimes ran out. People walked
to work and sometimes borrowed a
neighbor's shower. McKibbin called
the situation critical.

McKibbin was then asked to
prepare the nearby Bandelier
National Monument buildings
for overflow housing. Eighty more

Jumbo

The Babcock and Wilcox
Corporation of Barberton,
Ohio, built Jumbo, the
enormous steel container
for the bomb. Jumbo was
a safety measure. If the
bomb turned out to be a
dud, Jumbo needed to be
strong enough to with-
stand the conventional
explosives, so the scien-
tific team could rescue
the extremely valuable
plutonium for another try.
A special railroad flatcar
was built to transport the
casing from Ohio to New
Mexico. A specially built
64-wheel trailer then took
it by land to its desert destination, the test site.

people were arriving that summer of 1944, and they needed a place to live.

THE PROJECT PROGRESSES

By August, Los Alamos was bustling, and security was tighter than ever. Scientists were working day and night in a sort of urgent frenzy. Every afternoon, there were perhaps a half-dozen small explosions that growled in the distance and echoed in the canyons. People in Santa Fe heard them, but they did not refer to them as bombs or explosions. McKibbin and others described the rumblings as thunder and ignored the smoke that rose from the hills.

Oppenheimer was a different man now—driven, tormented, irritable, unfriendly, pessimistic, and thinner. Progress seemed to be at a standstill at Los Alamos. Oak Ridge—Site X—was not producing as much uranium as anticipated. Hanford was producing a fair amount of plutonium, but when

Nuclear Fallout

Fallout refers to the radioactive particles in the atmosphere after a nuclear explosion. These materials are called hot particles because they are radioactive—the nuclei of their atoms are unstable, losing energy by releasing electrons or other particles. Nuclear fallout can lead to contamination of the environment and the food chain, which can result in long-term external and internal exposure to radiation. This exposure can cause cancer and genetic damage.

some of it arrived at Los Alamos, it proved to be impure and unusable.

Preparations began to build the test bomb. It would be tested in a desolate area called Jornada del Muerto. The code name for the test, chosen by Oppenheimer, was Trinity. It was scheduled for July 1945.

A scientist at Los Alamos conducts research
as part of the Manhattan Project.

President Harry S. Truman

Not Over Yet

On April 12, 1945, Americans and the rest of the world were shocked at news that President Roosevelt had died. Vice President Harry Truman was now president of the United States. The war was not yet over. Residents of the

Hill especially were stunned. They had been working feverishly throughout the fall and winter on the bomb. Now, they wondered what would happen with the Manhattan Project. Bernice Brode, wife of one of the physicists, wrote about the day:

> When the news came over the loud speaker in the Tech Area, crowds gathered and everyone wondered what would become of the project now, since Truman, who would succeed to the presidency, did not know of our existence. A pall settled over our town.[1]

Within 24 hours of Roosevelt's death and being sworn in as president, Truman was told about the Manhattan Project and the atomic bomb. Work on the project continued without interruption.

Trinity Base Camp

Jumbo arrived in New Mexico that spring. Until it was ready to house the atomic device itself, Jumbo hung from a specially made tower in the desolate area of Jornada del Muerto. The site had been chosen from eight

Jornada del Muerto

Jornada del Muerto, is one of the roughest, most desolate desert areas of New Mexico. Land at the northern end is a lava field produced by a nearby volcano. The wide, flat valley, which offers no water or provisions for travelers for 100 miles (161 km), remains nearly uninhabited today.

The area gets its name from the days when Spanish wagon trains heading north would become stranded. The people died because they could find no water or provisions.

---

possible areas in the western United States as the best for the test. Kenneth Bainbridge was in charge of the test operation. Oppenheimer had set the target date for Trinity for sometime in July 1945.

Bainbridge designed the site, marking out ground zero and building from there. The pretest would take place 800 yards (732 m) from ground zero. Ten thousand yards (9,144 m) south of ground zero, a control bunker was planned, and another five miles (8 km) south of that was where the

Where to Test the Bomb

Eight sites were considered for Trinity, the testing of the atomic bomb:

- Tularosa Valley in southern New Mexico
- Jornada del Muerto in southern New Mexico
- The US Army's desert training area near Rice, California
- San Nicholas Island off the coast of Southern California
- The lava region south of Grants, New Mexico
- A New Mexico area southwest of Cuba and north of Thoreau
- Sandbars approximately ten miles (16 km) off the coast of southern Texas
- The San Luis Valley region near the Great Sand Dunes National Monument in southern Colorado

Bainbridge set five standards for the ideal test site. It had to be flat, with little dust, haze, or strong winds. It had to be remote, far from populated areas. It had to be isolated, unknown to most people, in order to ensure tight security. The site had to be somewhat close to Los Alamos to reduce transportation problems. Bainbridge's two top choices for the test site were Jornada del Muerto and the army's training area near Rice, California. He chose Jornada del Muerto because it was closer to Los Alamos and the government already owned the land.

base camp would be located. Laboratories went up, roads were built, and hundreds of miles of electrical wires were strung in preparation for the pretest.

Equipment and supplies arrived daily from Los Alamos and locations nationwide. Communication was established, although it was quite substandard. Telephone conversations were hard to understand, and telegraph service was poor. The best way to communicate was sending handwritten notes back and forth by truck.

Hundreds of scientists and project personnel moved to the area in a steady stream of cars, trucks, and buses. Security was extremely tight. Travelers to Trinity Base Camp were given directions along with strict instructions:

> *The following directions are strictly confidential and this copy is to be read by no one but yourself. You are to turn this copy in . . . on your return to the site.*[2]

It went on to say that they were not allowed, under any condition, to say they were connected with Santa Fe. Final instructions included the

Communication Blunder

Secure communication had to be set up at Trinity Base Camp. An exclusive short radio wave was requested. However, when first set up, it was the same frequency as the San Antonio, New Mexico, railroad. A ground to air system was also established. It, too, was initially unsecure. Its frequency was the same as the Voice of America, a radio station. As a result, thousands of people could hear their conversations.

directive: "Under no circumstances are telephone calls or stops for gasoline to be made between Albuquerque and your destination."[3]

On the way to the site, project members could only eat meals at a place called Roys in Belen, New Mexico. Once they arrived at the camp, they could not leave without special permission. They slept there and ate there, and they created their own entertainment. Going to nearby towns for dinner or a movie was prohibited. Outdoor movies at the camp were popular, and the army had an endless supply of Hollywood's best.

END OF THE WAR IN EUROPE

On May 7, 1945, Germany surrendered unconditionally. The war in Europe was over. But Japan, Germany's ally, refused to admit defeat. On June 8, Japanese officials resolved to continue the war in order to "protect the Imperial land, and accomplish the objectives for which we went to war."[4]

The first trial run of Trinity, a pretest, was scheduled in May. Hundreds of crates of explosives were stacked on a 20-foot (6-m) tower at the Trinity site. Tubes from Hanford with radioactive products were inserted into the pile. It resembled Chicago

Pile-1 underneath the university stadium, only it was larger. Even so, it was a small-scale test compared to what was to come. It was used to measure blast, earth shock, and remote damage.

The explosion went off before dawn on May 7. It was magnificent. A massive, bright fireball rose into the clear air, lighting up the dark sky. It could be seen as far away as Alamogordo, located 60 miles (97 km) southeast of the site. But as spectacular as the explosion was, it would pale in comparison to what would take place in a little more than two months. An exact date for Trinity had not yet been set.

INVASION OF JAPAN

On June 17, Truman wrote in his diary,

I have to decide Japanese strategy—shall we invade Japan proper or shall we bomb and blockade? That is my hardest decision to date. But I'll make it when I have all the facts.[5]

The next day, Truman held a meeting to discuss possible dates for the invasion of Japan. Military leaders at the meeting predicted hundreds of thousands of American casualties if the United States invaded

Massive Daily Deliveries

In May 1945, an average of 35 tons (32 metric tons) of supplies arrived daily at the Trinity site. By June, the average had risen to 54 tons (49 metric tons).

Japan. Dropping a bomb would save countless US lives.

The Manhattan Project was reaching its peak. The weapon designed to defeat Germany could be used to defeat Japan and completely end World War II. At the Trinity site, meteorologist J. M. Hubbard arrived to determine when the weather would be just right for detonating the test bomb. US Army Major T. O. Palmer stood ready with 160 of his enlisted men to evacuate cities in a 100-mile (161-km) radius, if it became necessary.

By July 12, the site had received enough plutonium for the bomb. Oppenheimer sent a coded telegram to two of his consultants:

> Anytime after the 15th would be a good time for our fishing trip. Because we are not certain of the weather we may be delayed several days. As we do not have enough sleeping bags to go around, we ask you please not to bring any one with you.[6]

Most of the scientists were working around the clock. The countdown to Trinity had begun.

Face Shields

A face shield was necessary at Trinity Base Camp. People with spare time made shields at the test site. The shields consisted of a piece of aluminum attached to a stick handle with welders' goggles for a window. They were designed to protect onlookers' eyes from the flash caused by the bomb's blast.

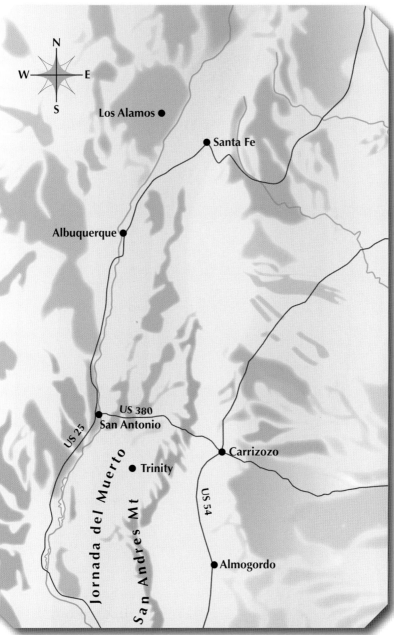

This map of New Mexico shows the location of Los Alamos
and the Trinity Test Site.

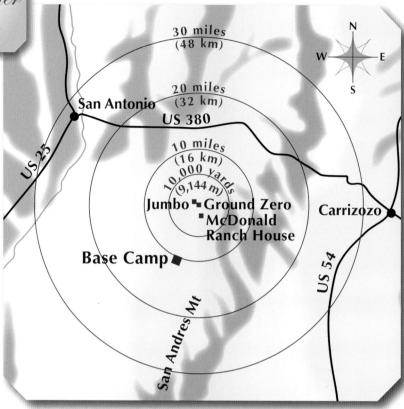

A drawing of the Trinity test site in New Mexico

TRINITY

t 3:00 p.m. on Thursday, July 12, 1945, a shipment of plutonium left Los Alamos in a car and headed for Trinity Base Camp. Nine hours later, explosive components of the bomb left Los Alamos by truck and made the trip to the site. On the afternoon of July 13, the bomb was assembled in a large canvas tent following step-by-step instructions written by Norris Bradbury:

Pick up GENTLY with hook.

Plug hole is covered with a CLEAN cloth.

Place hypodermic needle IN RIGHT PLACE. Check this carefully.

Insert HE—to be done as slowly as the G (Gadget) engineers wish. . . . Be sure shoe horn is on hand.

Sphere will be left overnight, cap up, in a small dish pan.[1]

TEST BOMB

The next morning, the tent was taken away. The bomb was hoisted to the top of the 100-foot (30-m) tower, where an armed guard watched it constantly. Target time for the test—zero hour—was approaching. It was scheduled for Monday, July 16, at 4:00 a.m., weather permitting. On Sunday evening, the sky was dark. Thunder rumbled in the nearby

Saying Good-bye

Before Oppenheimer left for the Trinity site, he said good-bye to his wife, Kitty. She pressed a four-leaf clover in his hand for good luck. He told her that if the test were successful, he would send her a little known line from a sonnet by French poet Charles Baudelaire: "You can change the sheets."[2]

mountains, and lightning flashed in the distant sky. At the camp, it was raining hard. Groves and Oppenheimer discussed the weather every five or ten minutes. They decided to postpone the test until the rain had stopped.

At 5:08 a.m., Bainbridge used his special key to unlock the protection around the switches. The countdown began at 5:09:45. Everyone took the required position: lying face down on the ground with his or her feet toward the blast. They closed their eyes and covered them with their hands. When there was a flash, they could turn over, if they chose to, and watch through the face shields they had been given. Groves later wrote about those moments:

> As we approached the final minute, the quiet grew more intense. I was on the ground (at Base Camp) between Bush and Conant. As I lay there in the final seconds, I thought only of what I would do if the countdown got to zero and nothing happened.[3]

People as far away as 200 miles (322 m), including scientists, their wives, a reporter, and military personnel, waited for the blast. In San Antonio, New Mexico, a restaurant owner was awakened by soldiers outside with seismographs. They told him, "If you come out in front of your store now, you'll see something the world has never seen before."[4] McKibbin sat in a car on top of Sandia Mountain in Albuquerque with a friend. She was gazing to the south and waiting for the spectacle.

With 45 seconds to go, a scientist flipped the switch that started the automatic timer.

Precious Cargo

The bomb's plutonium core was transported by car from the Hill to a location near Trinity Base Camp. To protect it from bumps and jolts, the plutonium was placed inside a carrying case surrounded with rubber bumpers and heavy wire. It rode in the backseat of an army car. Ahead of the car was another car with armed guards. Behind was a vehicle with specialists who would assemble the bomb.

Their destination was a ranch house owned by the McDonald family, who had been ordered to leave their home and property. The house was transformed into a clean room, a place that was thoroughly vacuumed and its windows sealed with black electrical tape to keep out dust. There, the assembly team put together the plutonium core of the bomb. On a table, the specialists spread out brown wrapping paper and carefully laid out the pieces of the bomb. The most important parts were two hemispheres of nickel-plated plutonium and several pieces of plum-colored uranium that weighed 80 pounds (36 kg).

US Army Brigadier General Thomas Farrell was asked to sign a receipt for the millions of dollars' worth of materials. Before he signed it, Farrell lifted the plutonium hemispheres in his hands. To his surprise, the plutonium was as warm as a living being.

Trinity was now out of human control. At minus ten seconds, physicist Ken Greisen called out, "Now I'm scared."[5] Sam Allison, the physicist counting down, shouted, "Now!"[6]

Gigantic Mushroom

The world's first atomic bomb exploded, vaporizing the tower and knocking over the 214-ton (194-metric ton) Jumbo. The sand around the tower melted and turned to a bright green glass. A huge blast of heat came that scorched the desert land. An incredibly bright orange and yellow fireball rose in the sky. It blossomed into a white ball that grew and spread into the shape of a gigantic mushroom. After 30 seconds or so, the white ball became a dull purple that rose about eight miles (13 km) into the air.

From her car, McKibbin saw the astonishing explosion. She recalled the event:

The feeling of awe that I had when that light hit us was remarkable. I don't think anyone has ever seen such an explosion. . . . The leaves of the green native trees were kind of shining with the gold. It was different. Everything was different. The world was changed.[7]

A photograph taken during Trinity shows the giant mushroom cloud that formed after the test bomb's detonation.

It would later be calculated that the blast equaled 18,000 tons (16,329 metric tons) of TNT and caused destruction one mile (1.6 km) in diameter.

A group of physicists jumped up and down around Oppenheimer, jubilantly slapping each other on the back and shrieking congratulations. But Oppenheimer was not as jubilant as the others. He walked outside and stared at what was now a column of smoke. He would later recall:

Eyewitness Account

A railroad engineer in Belen, New Mexico, was an eyewitness to Trinity's explosion. He described it as "a tremendous white flash. This was followed by a great red glare and high in the sky were three tremendous smoke rings. . . . They swirled and twisted as though being agitated by a great force."[10]

A few people laughed, a few people cried. Most people were silent. I remembered the line from the Hindu scripture, the Bhagavad Gita. . . . "I am become Death, the destroyer of worlds." I suppose we all thought that, one way or another.[8]

The only journalist allowed to witness Trinity was William L. Laurence of the *New York Times.* He would later write for the newspaper:

It was like the grand finale of a mighty symphony of the elements, fascinating and terrifying, uplifting and crushing, ominous, devastating, full of great promise and great foreboding. . . . On that moment hung eternity. Time stood still. Space contracted to a pinpoint. It was as though the earth had opened and the skies split. One felt as though he had been privileged to witness the Birth of the World—to be present at the moment of Creation when the Lord said: Let there be light.[9]

Shortly after Trinity's blast, Enrico Fermi went to the blast site to gather information and soil samples. There, he found a 1,200-foot (366-m) crater and a few charred remnants of the steel tower.

News Flash

Immediately, calls from residents started coming in to the local radio station. The announcer quickly made an announcement to quell people's fears:

FLASH! The explosives dump at the Alamogordo Air Base has blown up. No lives are lost. The explosion is what caused the tremendous sound and the light in the sky. I repeat for the benefit of the many phone calls coming in: the explosive dump at the Alamogordo Air Base has blown up. No lives are lost.[11]

The *Santa Fe New Mexican* newspaper published the same story on the back page and reported that an ammunition magazine had blown up. Another newspaper attributed the blast to lightning. Meanwhile, the army prepared a statement to answer questions about this huge explosion:

A remotely located ammunition magazine containing a considerable amount of high explosives and pyrotechnics exploded. There was no loss of life or injury to anyone, and the property damage outside of the explosives magazine itself was negligible.

Getting to Ground Zero

Fermi planned to take a tank to the blast site to test the soil after the explosion. He climbed into a lead-lined army tank that would protect him from radioactive fallout, but the tank never made it to ground zero. On the way to the blast site, the tank broke down under its own weight, so Fermi got out and went on foot. Nine years later, Fermi died from stomach cancer that may have been caused by his work with radioactive materials.

Weather conditions affecting the content of gas shells exploded by the blast may make it desirable for the Army to evacuate temporarily a few civilians from their homes.[12]

The statement was printed in New Mexico newspapers and aired on West Coast radio. Most people believed it. The federal government's Office of Censorship made sure the real facts were not printed in newspapers in the Eastern United States. A coded message was sent to US Secretary of War Henry L. Stimson:

Operated on this morning. Diagnosis not yet complete but results seem satisfactory and already exceed expectations. Local press release necessary as interest extends a great distance. Dr. Groves pleased. He returns tomorrow. I will keep you posted.[13]

Visiting the Test Site

The Trinity Test Site was declared a national historic landmark on December 21, 1965. The site is open to the public twice a year, in April and October.

Meanwhile, exhausted scientists returned to Los Alamos. The next day, people were celebrating in the streets of the Hill with parades, parties, and two fingers held up in a V for victory. Their work was not yet done, however. The war was not over.

Oppenheimer, left, and Groves view what was left of the tower after the detonation and massive explosion of their test bomb.

The ground crew of the Enola Gay *stands with pilot Paul Tibbets Jr., center. The B-29 bomber dropped the first nuclear weapon used in warfare, the atomic bomb Little Boy, on Hiroshima, Japan, on August 6, 1945.*

LITTLE BOY AND FAT MAN

When the Trinity test bomb went off in New Mexico, President Truman was in Potsdam, Germany, meeting with Winston Churchill and Russian leader Joseph Stalin. From July 17 to August 2, 1945, the men discussed how to demand a

Japanese surrender. The success of the atomic bomb test provided them with a possible solution to a war that seemed as though it would never end.

Even as Trinity was detonating, another bomb—an atomic bomb called "Little Boy"—was being loaded onto the naval cruiser USS *Indianapolis* in California's San Francisco Bay. It arrived at the Pacific island of Tinian on July 26, 1945, minus its nuclear parts. Two days later, five C-54 cargo planes arrived with those parts. Little Boy, the world's second nuclear bomb, was ready for use. Truman and Churchill approved a November 1 deadline for the invasion of Japan. Truman gave the go-ahead to use the atomic bomb after August 3, weather permitting.

A committee had been formed to come up with a list of suggested Japanese cities to bomb. Four targets were finally approved: Hiroshima, Kokura, Niigata, and Nagasaki. Hiroshima was the headquarters for

Surrender Equaled Shame

Japanese soldiers were taught that surrender was shameful to their families and country. They preferred suicide to surrender. Joseph Grew was once a US ambassador to Japan and had lived in Japan for ten years. He wrote, "The Japanese will not crack. . . . Only by utter physical destruction or utter exhaustion of their men and materials can they be defeated."[1]

Japan's army and a major military storage location. The city would be the first target, where the bomb would most severely damage the Japanese military.

Hiroshima

On July 26, the day Little Boy arrived at Tinian, Truman issued to Japan what came to be called the Potsdam Declaration:

> *Land, sea and air forces of the United States, the British Empire and of China . . . are poised to strike the final blows upon Japan. . . . The full application of our military power, backed by our resolve, WILL mean the inevitable and complete destruction of the Japanese armed forces and just as inevitably the utter destruction of the Japanese homeland. . . . We call upon the Government of Japan to proclaim now the unconditional surrender of all Japanese armed forces. . . . The alternative for Japan is prompt and utter destruction.* [2]

Japan rejected the terms of the declaration. On August 6, 1945, at 2:45 a.m., US Air Force Colonel Paul Tibbets Jr. boarded a B-29 bomber dubbed *Enola Gay*. He departed Tinian Island with 11 crew members and headed to Hiroshima. On board was the atomic bomb Little Boy, which weighed 9,700 pounds (4,400 kg). The total weight of the plane that day was 65 tons (59 metric tons), well over its maximum. At 3:00 a.m., crew members started assembling the bomb in the cramped quarters of the bomb bay. One of the crew asked Tibbets, "Colonel, are we splitting atoms today?" Tibbets gave him a strange look and said, "That's about it."[3]

At 7:30 a.m. Tinian time, weapons expert Deak Parsons dropped down to the bomb bay to arm Little Boy. He pulled out the green plugs and inserted red ones, which activated the bomb's internal batteries. As the plane approached its target, the

Naming the *Enola Gay*

The B-29 bomber that carried Little Boy was dubbed *Enola Gay* by pilot Paul Tibbets Jr. He named it the day before he flew it over Hiroshima. Enola Gay Tibbets was his mother, who had assured him that he would not be killed while flying. Tibbets had always remembered his mother's words when he got into a tight spot in a plane. Before he took off, he located a sign painter, handed him a piece of paper with his mother's name on it, and told him to "paint that on the strike ship, nice and big."[4] The square, 12-inch- (22-cm-) high letters were painted directly underneath the pilot's window.

Pilot Robert Lewis had often flown the B-29. To his disappointment, he was the co-pilot for this mission. When Lewis saw *Enola Gay* painted on the plane, he was furious and shouted his disapproval. He stomped off to find Tibbets. Since Tibbets outranked him, Lewis was overruled.

In 1995, the cockpit and nose section of the *Enola Gay* was exhibited at the National Air and Space Museum of the Smithsonian Institution in Washington DC. In 2003, after years of work restoring the plane, it was put on display at the museum's new Steven F. Udvar-Hazy Center.

Escort Aircraft

The *Enola Gay* was escorted by two other B-29 bombers: the *Great Artiste*, commanded by Major Charles W. Sweeney, and a nameless aircraft that was later called *Necessary Evil*. The second plane, commanded by Major George Marquardt, carried the equipment and photographers who captured pictures of the explosion.

crew donned heavy body armor and protective goggles. The doors of the bomb bay were open. Little Boy's clock was ticking. At just the right moment, the bomb dropped from the plane.

At 9:16 a.m. Tinian time (8:16 a.m. Hiroshima time), on August 6, 1945, Little Boy exploded midair, 1,900 feet (580 m) above the city of Hiroshima, just 43 seconds after it fell from the *Enola Gay*. There was a blinding flash and then a giant fireball that sent surface temperatures to 5,400 degrees Fahrenheit (2,982°C). Fierce heat rays and radiation burst in every direction, unleashing a high-pressure shockwave. It killed tens of thousands of people and animals, melted buildings and streetcars, and reduced a 400-year-old city to dust.

The *Enola Gay* jolted at the blast. Tibbets recalled the event:

A bright light filled the plane. The first shock wave hit us. We were eleven and a half miles . . . from the atomic explosion, but the whole airplane cracked and crinkled from the blast.

. . . When the second wave came, he [the tail gunner] called out a warning. We turned back to look at Hiroshima. The city was hidden by that awful cloud . . . boiling up, mushrooming, terrible and incredibly tall. . . . Lewis said he could taste atomic fission. He said it tasted like lead.[5]

Robert Lewis wrote in a journal, "I'll never quite get these few minutes out of my mind."[6]

At 11:00 a.m. Santa Fe time, Dorothy McKibbin heard a news bulletin on a radio in her office at 109 East Palace. It was President Truman's voice:

Sixteen hours ago an American airplane dropped one bomb on Hiroshima, an important Japanese army base. That bomb had more power than 20,000 tons of T.N.T. . . . It is an atomic bomb. It is a harnessing of the basic power of the universe. The force from which the sun draws its power has been loosed against those who brought war to the Far East.[7]

Hiroshima Casualties

Some 80,000 Japanese citizens were killed in the first few seconds of the atomic bomb explosion. More than 62,000 buildings were destroyed. By the end of 1945, the number of deaths had risen to approximately 100,000. Approximately five years after the bombing, the death total probably exceeded 200,000 due to cancer and other long-term effects of radiation.

It was the largest bomb in the history of warfare, in the history of the world. But it would not be the last.

Fat Man was the second atomic bomb dropped
by US servicemen over Japan.

Japan Refuses to Surrender

Even after the massive damage to Hiroshima,
Japan refused to surrender. Truman warned the
Japanese that the United States would attack other
cities with similar devastating results. US airplanes
showered millions of leaflets all over Japan, warning
the people:

> *We are in possession of the most destructive explosive ever
> devised by man. . . . This awful fact is one for you to ponder
> and we solemnly assure you it is grimly accurate. We have just
> begun to use this weapon against your homeland.*[8]

On August 9, at 3:47 a.m., a B-29 bomber
named *Bock's Car*, after its commander Captain
Frederick C. Bock, took off from Tinian Island.
The plane, piloted that day by Major Charles W.
Sweeney, headed to a weapons factory near the city
of Kokura, Japan. The plane carried a plutonium
implosion bomb called "Fat Man." Ten minutes
into the mission, the bomb's little green plugs were
changed to red ones. The bomb was fully armed.

NAGASAKI

The plane encountered problem after problem.
The pilot was unable to access the reserve fuel tank.
One of the two escort B-29s never arrived. The air
was smoky and hazy, and there was no sign of the
target city, Kokura. *Bock's Car* turned to its second
target: the city of Nagasaki. Clouds obscured the
crew's view of that city as well. But the bomb was
already armed, and Sweeney did not want to take the
bomb back home or drop it in the ocean.

Finally, a crew member caught a glimpse of the
city of Nagasaki through the clouds. Fat Man was
dropped out of the plane. It was 11:02 a.m. when
the bomb exploded over Nagasaki. The explosion
was 40 percent stronger than the blast of Little Boy,

although the damage would be less severe because of the surrounding terrain.

In spite of the warning leaflets dropped earlier, there were still approximately 200,000 people in the city. No one knows for certain how many died as a result of the bomb, but estimates are that some 40,000 casualties occurred from the initial blast.

Japanese Surrender

Truman ordered a stop to atomic bombing. On August 14, 1945, Japanese Emperor Michinomiya Hirohito overruled Japan's military leaders and forced them to surrender unconditionally. He accepted the Potsdam Declaration, so long as it did not affect his position as sovereign ruler of Japan. World War II was finally over.

On August 15, the emperor's surrender speech was broadcast over the radio. It was the first time the Japanese people had ever heard their leader's treble voice. The emperor said he was "willing to endure the unendurable, tolerate the intolerable, for peace to last thousands of generations."[9]

"If atomic bombs are to be added as new weapons to the arsenals of a warring world, or to the arsenals of nations preparing for war, then the time will come when mankind will curse the names of Los Alamos and Hiroshima."[10]

—J. Robert Oppenheimer, October 16, 1945

As was the case with the test bomb in New Mexico, the atomic bomb that was dropped over Hiroshima, Japan, resulted in a giant mushroom cloud.

*The atomic bombs dropped by the United States on Japan in 1945
caused tens of thousands of deaths and massive destruction.*

AFTERMATH

The bombings of Hiroshima and Nagasaki brought many Manhattan Project scientists and workers guilt and misgivings. Oppenheimer was especially remorseful, writing numerous letters of reflection over the next few weeks.

The future of the world and of Los Alamos was unknown. The number of technical staff dropped dramatically. Many who thought the site would be abandoned went back to their previous jobs as researchers and university professors. Brilliant physicists such as Enrico Fermi and Edward Teller returned to the University of Chicago, where the idea of the atomic bomb had begun. Others felt strongly that Los Alamos should be shut down or transformed into a peacetime research facility. Oppenheimer resigned his position as director and went to work for Princeton University. He appointed Norris Bradbury as temporary director of the Los Alamos laboratory.

Edward Teller

Edward Teller authored more than a dozen books, mostly about nuclear energy and defense. In 1975, Teller became senior research fellow at the Hoover Institute for the Study of War, Revolution, and Peace at Stanford University in Stanford, California. He died in 2003 at the age of 95.

A PERMANENT LOS ALAMOS

Bradbury suggested that Los Alamos become a peacetime laboratory focused on the study of nuclear energy. However, he added that the "project cannot neglect the stockpiling or the development of atomic weapons in this interim period."[1] General Groves added to the stability of the site by approving construction of the first permanent housing.

In August 1946, the US Congress passed the McMahon Act, which created the Atomic Energy Commission (AEC). Although nuclear weapons were still being tested, a second focus—nuclear energy— improved public opinion of Los Alamos and paved the way for nuclear power sources.

Los Alamos maintained its active research into atomic weapons. In January 1950, Truman made a declaration:

> It is part of my responsibility as Commander-in-Chief to see to it that our country is able to defend itself against any possible aggressor. Accordingly, I have directed the Atomic Energy Commission to continue its work on all forms of atomic weapons, including the so-called hydrogen or super-bomb.[2]

THE COLD WAR

During the Cold War (1945–1991), the Soviet Union and the United States were in conflict. Although there were no direct military battles between the superpowers, there was a competition for political power that included a race to obtain the most powerful nuclear weapons.

In 1949, Truman revealed that the Soviet Union had tested a nuclear weapon. Consequently, the United States increased its research of a new bomb: the hydrogen bomb. In 1952, seven years after the bombing of Hiroshima and Nagasaki, Japan, there was an enormous explosion. A test bomb sent a fireball three miles (4.8 km) wide into the air, followed by a gigantic mushroom cloud over the Pacific Ocean.

The code name of the bomb was "Mike." It was a hydrogen bomb—the H-bomb. It yielded the equivalent of 10.4 million tons (9.4 metric tons) of TNT, a thousand times more powerful than Little Boy. It completely destroyed the island Elugelab, where it was detonated, leaving a crater one-half mile (.8 km) deep and two miles (3.2 km) wide in the reef. Teller, who had returned to Los Alamos in 1950 to work on the H-bomb, would come to be known as the "Father of the Hydrogen Bomb."

The Nuclear Club

Since the end of World War II, other nations have developed nuclear weapons and technology. As of 2010, eight political powers have successfully developed nuclear weapons: the United States, the United Kingdom, Russia, France, China, India, North Korea, and Pakistan. Israel is believed to have nuclear weapons but this has not been confirmed.

Target of McCarthyism

Many scientists who had worked on Little Boy and Fat Man condemned the hydrogen bomb. Oppenheimer voiced his opposition. This, along with his past left wing, communist ties, stirred suspicion against Oppenheimer. The man whose picture had appeared on covers of *Time* magazine and *Physics Today* was now the object of misgiving. His phones were tapped, his mail was seized, and his office and home were bugged. Government agents followed and watched him wherever he went. After years of surveillance, Oppenheimer's security clearance was suspended because of his

Spy from Los Alamos

Klaus Fuchs was a Communist who immigrated to Edinburgh, Scotland, from Germany in 1933 to escape the Nazis. He studied physics at the University of Bristol, where he earned his doctorate. In 1943, Fuchs joined the Manhattan Project as a member of the group of scientists Winston Churchill sent from Great Britain to help with the project. Initially, the physicist was assigned to work at Columbia University in New York City. He was later moved to Site Y in Los Alamos, New Mexico.

Upon arriving at Los Alamos, Fuchs began filtering classified US information to the Soviet Union, but his actions were not discovered until 1949. The physicist admitted to spying for the Soviets in January 1950, which the Soviet Union denied. He was convicted in March and sentenced to prison for 14 years. Fuchs was released on June 23, 1959. He moved to Dresden, East Germany, after his release. There, he worked as a scientist. Klaus Fuchs died in East Germany on January 28, 1988.

associations with Communists in the 1930s. He was criticized and mistrusted for his opposition to the development of the hydrogen bomb.

Oppenheimer found himself the target in a political climate of the time known as McCarthyism. Many Americans fell under the suspicious eye of Senator Joseph R. McCarthy, chairman of the Senate Permanent Subcommittee on Investigations. Oppenheimer requested a hearing in 1954 before the AEC to get his security clearance restored. The most condemning testimony at the hearing came from Los Alamos colleague Edward Teller, who testified at the hearing:

> *In a great number of cases I have seen Dr. Oppenheimer act—I understand that Dr. Oppenheimer has acted—in a way that for me was extremely hard to understand. I thoroughly disagree with him in numerous issues and his actions frankly appeared to me confused and complicated. To this extent I feel that I would like to see the vital interests of this country in hands which I understand better and therefore trust more. In this very limited sense I would like to express a feeling that I would feel personally more secure if public matters would rest in other hands.*[3]

Oppenheimer in 1950

Teller was asked if it would be a danger to the country's defense and security if Oppenheimer had security clearance. Teller responded that "if it is a question of wisdom and judgment, as demonstrated by actions since 1945, then I would say one would be wiser not to grant clearance."[4] Oppenheimer's fate was sealed; the AEC voted 4–1 to continue to deny Oppenheimer security clearance. They cited as their main reasons Oppenheimer's unreliable character and questionable loyalty. The man who had coordinated the Manhattan Project and given the atomic bomb to the United States returned to Princeton University under a cloud of suspicion. He could no longer give official advice on atomic energy or the atomic bomb he helped create. He no longer had access to Los Alamos, the laboratory he had founded.

Teller gained favor with some government agencies, but many in his own scientific community rejected and scorned him for testifying against Oppenheimer. Thirty years later, McKibbin was asked about Oppenheimer and Teller in a television interview. She compared them to an orchid (Oppenheimer) and a dandelion (Teller). She explained of the two men:

Making Amends

In 1963, US President John F. Kennedy attempted to restore the broken relationship with Oppenheimer by granting him the Fermi Award for scientific achievement. Kennedy was assassinated that year, and President Lyndon Johnson presented the award to Oppenheimer. Oppenheimer died three years later. Decades after his passing, Oppenheimer is still respected by those who worked with him and revered as a legend by scientists who have followed in his footsteps to research nuclear energy.

You can't compare their characters any more than you can compare an orchid to a dandelion. . . . An orchid is more finely designed, and built, and delicate, and subtle, and aromatic. And a dandelion is something you kick up with the heel of your shoe if it's going to take over your grass.[5]

HISTORY WILL NOT FORGET

What began as the Manhattan Project underneath a football stadium in Chicago grew into a worldwide nuclear weapons program. History will not forget the people who were the project: J. Robert Oppenheimer, Enrico Fermi, Kenneth Bainbridge, Leslie Groves, Dorothy McKibbin, and so many more. They were the brains, the heart, and the passion of the Manhattan Project. The work they contributed to amazing scientific discoveries not only split the tiny atom but ended a worldwide war. And their breakthroughs opened up a new world: the world of the atom, of its nucleus, of its nuclear power, its nuclear energy, and nuclear weapons.

"[The Manhattan Project was] a time that was tragic, ironic and epic, all three, but most of all intensely human, and compelled from the beginning not by malice or hatred but by hope for a better world."[6]

—*Richard Rhodes, Pulitzer Prize winner for* The Making of the Atomic Bomb

The Los Alamos National Laboratory's Bradbury Science Museum has a variety of information about the Manhattan Project and Site Y.

TIMELINE

1938	1939	1940
German chemists Otto Hahn and Fritz Strassmann bombard a uranium atom with neutrons, causing nuclear fission.	On October 21, the Advisory Committee on Uranium meets for the first time in Washington DC.	Britain's MAUD Committee meets for the first time on April 10 to research the uranium bomb.

1942	1942	1942
In August, the United States creates the Manhattan Engineer District, often referred to as the Manhattan Project, in New York City.	Land is purchased in Oak Ridge, Tennessee, in September for Site X to study uranium.	J. Robert Oppenheimer is appointed scientific head of the Manhattan Project in October.

1941

The MAUD Committee gives its bomb project to the United States in July.

1941

The United States begins expanded research in atomic energy on December 6.

1941

Japan attacks Pearl Harbor, Hawaii, on December 7; the next day, the United States declares war on Japan and enters World War II.

1942

On December 2, physicist Enrico Fermi achieves a nuclear chain reaction at the University of Chicago.

1943

Construction begins on Site Y in Los Alamos, New Mexico, in January.

1943

Dorothy Scarritt McKibbin is hired in March as the gatekeeper of Site Y.

TIMELINE

1943	1943	1944
Site Y—Los Alamos, the Hill—officially opens on April 15.	Britain's top scientists arrive in Los Alamos in the fall.	Focus moves from the Thin Man nuclear weapon to Little Boy.

1945	1945	1945
On June 18, President Truman discusses possible dates for the invasion of Japan.	Trinity Base Camp receives the plutonium explosive components for a bomb on July 12.	The first atomic bomb explodes on July 16 at Jornada del Muerto in New Mexico.

1945	1945	1945
Location is chosen and base camp is constructed for Trinity, the testing of the atomic bomb.	President Roosevelt dies on April 12, and Harry Truman becomes president.	Germany surrenders unconditionally on May 7, ending the war in Europe.

1945	1945	1945
Atomic bomb Little Boy explodes over Hiroshima, Japan, on August 6.	Atomic bomb Fat Man explodes over Nagasaki, Japan, on August 9.	Japan surrenders on August 14, ending World War II.

ESSENTIAL FACTS

DATE OF EVENT

August 1942–August 1945

PLACES OF EVENT

New York City, New York

Los Alamos, New Mexico

Oak Ridge, Tennessee

Wendover, Utah

Hanford, Washington

Hiroshima and Nagasaki, Japan

KEY PLAYERS

❖ Enrico Fermi, physicist

❖ Leslie Groves, US Army general

❖ Michinomiya Hirohito, emperor of Japan

❖ Adolf Hitler, Führer and chancellor of Germany

❖ J. Robert Oppenheimer, physicist

❖ Franklin D. Roosevelt, president of the United States

❖ Harry S. Truman, president of the United States

The Manhattan Project

Highlights of Event

❖ On September 1, 1939, Germany invaded Poland, sparking World War II.

❖ Japanese bombers attacked Pearl Harbor, Hawaii, on December 7, 1941, pulling the United States into World War II the following day, when war is declared on Japan.

❖ In August 1942, the United States created the Manhattan Engineer District, often referred to as the Manhattan Project, in New York City to study nuclear fission. The purpose of the project was to make a nuclear weapon before Germany did.

❖ In September 1942, US Army General Leslie Groves was placed in charge of the Manhattan Project, and he appointed J. Robert Oppenheimer as scientific head of the mission. Oppenheimer convinced Groves to build a secret site in New Mexico where scientists could converge and work together on a nuclear weapon.

❖ Site Y, located in Los Alamos, New Mexico, opened on April 15, 1943. The world's top scientists began working on creating the first nuclear bomb.

❖ The world's first atomic bomb was detonated on July 16, 1945, at a remote area of New Mexico called Jornada del Muerto. Trinity was the code name for this successful testing of a nuclear bomb.

❖ In August 1945, two atomic bombs—Little Boy and Fat Man—were exploded over the Japanese cities of Hiroshima and Nagasaki, bringing an end to World War II.

Quote

"A few people laughed, a few people cried. Most people were silent. I remembered the line from the Hindu scripture, the Bhagavad Gita. . . . 'I am become Death, the destroyer of worlds.' I suppose we all thought that, one way or another."—*J. Robert Oppenheimer, in response to Trinity*

Glossary

atomic
Relating to an atom or atoms; using nuclear energy.

critical
In nuclear fission, the steady state when there is no increase in neutrons, power, or temperature.

detonate
To cause to explode.

fallout
Radioactive particles created when a nuclear weapon explodes.

isotope
Atoms with the same number of protons in the nucleus but a different number of neutrons.

mesa
An elevated area of land with a flat top and sides, usually with steep cliffs.

metallurgist
A scientist who studies the procedures used to extract and purify metals from their ores.

neutron
The particle of the nucleus of an atom with no electric charge.

nuclear fission
The act of splitting a nucleus of an atom, usually into two parts.

physics
The branch of science concerned with the relationship between matter and energy.

plutonium
A toxic radioactive metallic element produced artificially by neutron bombardment of uranium.

prefabricated
Built in a factory and transported to a construction site.

radioactive
    The unstable state of an atom's nucleus during decay or change.

seismograph
    An instrument used to measure and record the size and force of waves traveling through earth, often as a result of an explosion or earthquake.

stockpiling
    Storing resources.

TNT
    Trinitrotoluene, a yellow compound used mainly as a high explosive.

uranium
    A heavy metallic element that is radioactive and toxic.

ADDITIONAL RESOURCES

SELECTED BIBLIOGRAPHY

Bird, Kai, and Martin J. Sherwin. *American Prometheus: The Triumph and Tragedy of J. Robert Oppenheimer*. New York: Random House, 2005. Print.

Conant, Jennet. *109 East Palace: Robert Oppenheimer and the Secret City of Los Alamos*. New York: Simon & Schuster, 2005. Print.

Kelly, Cynthia C., ed. *The Manhattan Project: The Birth of the Atomic Bomb in the Words of Its Creators, Eyewitnesses, and Historians*. New York: Black Dog & Leventhal, 2007. Print.

Los Alamos Scientific Laboratory Public Relations. *Los Alamos: Beginning of an Era 1943–1945*. Los Alamos, NM: Los Alamos Historical Society, 1999. Print.

Rhodes, Richard. *The Making of the Atomic Bomb*. New York: Simon & Schuster, 1986. Print.

Steeper, Nancy Cook. *Dorothy Scarritt McKibbin: Gatekeeper to Los Alamos*. Los Alamos, NM: Los Alamos Historical Society, 2003. Print.

FURTHER READINGS

Allman, Toney. *J. Robert Oppenheimer: Theoretical Physicist, Atomic Pioneer*. Detroit, MI: Thomson Gale, 2005. Print.

Elish, Dan. *The Manhattan Project*. New York: Children's, 2008. Print.

Web Links

To learn more about the Manhattan Project, visit ABDO Publishing Company online at **www.abdopublishing.com**. Web sites about the Manhattan Project are featured on our Book Links page. These links are routinely monitored and updated to provide the most current information available.

Places to Visit

Bradbury Science Museum, Los Alamos National Laboratory
1350 Central Avenue, Los Alamos, NM 87544
505-667-4444
The museum's exhibits detail the history of Los Alamos National Laboratory, including its research, which encompasses a variety of sciences. Several exhibits are interactive.

Los Alamos Historical Museum
1050 Bathtub Row, Post Office Box 43, Los Alamos, NM 87544
505-662-6272
www.losalamoshistory.org
In addition to life during the Manhattan Project, exhibits explore the geology and archaeology of the Los Alamos area, the homesteading period, the Los Alamos Ranch School, and interaction with locals.

The National Museum of Nuclear Science & History
601 Eubank Boulevard SE, Albuquerque, NM 87123
505-245-2137
Exhibits feature the past, present, and future of nuclear science, from the origins of atomic theory, the political scenes of World War II and the Cold War, and modern-day advances in nuclear medicine.

Source Notes

Chapter 1. Gatekeeper to Los Alamos

1. Kai Bird and Martin J. Sherwin. *American Prometheus: The Triumph and Tragedy of J. Robert Oppenheimer*. New York: Random House, 2005. 214. Print.

2. Nancy Cook Steeper. *Dorothy Scarritt McKibbin: Gatekeeper to Los Alamos*. Los Alamos, NM: Los Alamos Historical Society, 2003. 1. Print.

3. Ibid.

Chapter 2. The Manhattan Project

1. "Letter from Albert Einstein to President Franklin Delano Roosevelt." 2 Aug. 1939. *PBS.org*. Public Broadcasting Service, 2010. Web. 17 Sept. 2010.

2. "FDR – Albert Einstein – 10/19/39." *Franklin D. Roosevelt Presidential Library and Museum*. Marist College, n.d. Web. 2 Nov. 2009.

3. "Vannevar Bush and Ernest Lawrence – Two Key Individuals." *Y12.doe.gov*. B&W Y-12, 2010. Web. 17 Sept. 2010.

4. "Order Establishing the National Defense Research Committee." *Franklin D. Roosevelt Presidential Library and Museum*. Marist College, n.d. Web. 2 Nov. 2009.

5. Richard Rhodes. *The Making of the Atomic Bomb*. New York: Simon & Schuster, 1986. 406. Print.

6. "Albert Einstein 1879–1955." *OxfordReference.com*. Oxford University Press, 2010. Web. 17 Sept. 2010.

Chapter 3. Sites X and Y

1. Richard Rhodes. *The Making of the Atomic Bomb*. New York: Simon & Schuster, 1986. 440. Print.

2. Ibid. 12.

3. "CP-1 Goes Critical." *Doe.gov*. US Department of Energy, n.d. Web. 17 Sept. 2010.

4. Ibid.

5. "History of the Los Alamos Ranch School." *LosAlamosHistory.org*. Los Alamos Historical Society, n.d. Web. 2 Nov. 2009.

6. Nancy Cook Steeper. *Dorothy Scarritt McKibbin: Gatekeeper to Los Alamos*. Los Alamos, NM: Los Alamos Historical Society, 2003. 68. Print.

7. Richard Rhodes. *The Making of the Atomic Bomb*. New York: Simon & Schuster, 1986. 440. Print.

8. Ibid. 452.

9. *Los Alamos: Beginning of an Era 1943–1945*. Los Alamos, NM: Los Alamos Historical Society, 1999. 12. Print.

10. Nobel Web AB. "The Nobel Prize in Physics in 1938." *Nobelprize.org*. Nobel Web Ab, 2009. Web. 26 Dec. 2009.

Chapter 4. Life on the Hill

1. *Los Alamos: Beginning of an Era 1943–1945*. Los Alamos, NM: Los Alamos Historical Society, 1999. 12. Print.

2. Ferenc Morton Szasz. *The Day the Sun Rose Twice: The Story of the Trinity Site Nuclear Explosion, July 16*, 1945. Albuquerque: University of New Mexico Press, 1984. 22. Print.

3. *Los Alamos: Beginning of an Era 1943–1945*. Los Alamos, NM: Los Alamos Historical Society, 1999. 18. Print.

4. Ferenc Morton Szasz. *The Day the Sun Rose Twice: The Story of the Trinity Site Nuclear Explosion, July 16*, 1945. Albuquerque: University of New Mexico Press, 1984. 21. Print.

5. Los Alamos Scientific Laboratory Public Relations. *Los Alamos: Beginning of an Era 1943–1945*. Los Alamos, NM: Los Alamos Historical Society, 1999. 18. Print.

Chapter 5. Two Weapons

1. Dan Kurzman. *The Day of the Bomb: Countdown to Hiroshima*. New York: McGraw-Hill, 1986. 160. Print.

Chapter 6. Not Over Yet

1. Nancy Cook Steeper. *Dorothy Scarritt McKibbin: Gatekeeper to Los Alamos*. Los Alamos, NM: Los Alamos Historical Society, 2003. 105. Print.

2. Los Alamos Scientific Laboratory Public Relations. *Los Alamos: Beginning of an Era 1943–1945*. Los Alamos, NM: Los Alamos Historical Society, 1999. 38. Print.

3. Ibid.

4. Robert James Maddox. "The Biggest Decision: Why We Had to Drop the Atomic Bomb." *NIU.edu*. Board of Trustees of Northern Illinois University, May/June 1995. Web. 18 Sept. 2009.

5. Ibid.

6. Los Alamos Scientific Laboratory Public Relations. *Los Alamos: Beginning of an Era 1943–1945*. Los Alamos, NM: Los Alamos Historical Society, 1999. 46. Print.

Source Notes Continued

Chapter 7. Trinity

1. Los Alamos Scientific Laboratory Public Relations. *Los Alamos: Beginning of an Era 1943–1945.* Los Alamos, NM: Los Alamos Historical Society, 1999. 47. Print.

2. Lansing Lamont. "Oppie: The Troubled Pied Piper of Los Alamos." *Life.* 3 March 1967. 34B. Print.

3. Los Alamos Scientific Laboratory Public Relations. *Los Alamos: Beginning of an Era 1943–1945.* 2nd ed., Los Alamos, NM: Los Alamos Historical Society. 51. Print.

4. Ibid. 50.

5. "The Trinity Test." *DOE.gov.* US Department of Energy, n.d. Web. 2 Nov. 2009.

6. Ibid.

7. Jennet Conant. *109 East Palace: Robert Oppenheimer and the Secret City of Los Alamos.* New York: Simon & Schuster, 2005. 312. Print.

8. Ibid.

9. Los Alamos Scientific Laboratory Public Relations. *Los Alamos: Beginning of an Era 1943–1945.* Los Alamos, NM: Los Alamos Historical Society, 1999. 53–54. Print.

10. Ferenc Morton Szasz. *The Day the Sun Rose Twice: The Story of the Trinity Site Nuclear Explosion July 16, 1945.* Albuquerque: University of New Mexico Press, 1984. 85–86. Print.

11. Jennet Conant. *109 East Palace: Robert Oppenheimer and the Secret City of Los Alamos.* New York: Simon & Schuster, 2005. 313–314. Print.

12. Richard Rhodes. *The Making of the Atomic Bomb.* New York: Simon & Schuster, 1986. 685–686. Print.

13. Jennet Conant. *109 East Palace: Robert Oppenheimer and the Secret City of Los Alamos.* New York: Simon & Schuster, 2005. 314. Print.

Chapter 8. Little Boy and Fat Man

1. Richard Rhodes. *The Making of the Atomic Bomb*. New York: Simon & Schuster, 1986. 520. Print.

2. "The Japanese Surrender Documents – WWII." Ibiblio.org. *National Public Telecomputing Network, Purdue University, n.d.* Web. 2 Nov. 2009.

3. Richard Rhodes. *The Making of the Atomic Bomb*. New York: Simon & Schuster, 1986. 707. Print.

4. Ibid. 711.

5. Ibid. 710.

6. Ibid. 711.

7. Jennet Conant. *109 East Palace: Robert Oppenheimer and the Secret City of Los Alamos*. New York: Simon & Schuster, 2005. 323–324. Print.

8. "The Atomic Bombing of Hiroshima." *DOE.gov*. US Department of Energy, n.d. Web. 18 Sept. 2009.

9. "Emperor Hirohito Surrenders to the Allies." *History.com*. A&E Television Networks, 2010. Web. 17 Sept. 2010.

10. Kai Bird and Martin J. Sherwin. *American Prometheus: The Triumph and Tragedy of J. Robert Oppenheimer*. New York: Knopf, 2005. 323. Print.

Chapter 9. Aftermath

1. Rhodes, R. *Dark Sun: The Making of the Hydrogen Bomb*. New York: Simon and Schuster, 1995. 212. Print.

2. Los Alamos Scientific Laboratory Public Relations. *Los Alamos: Beginning of an Era 1943–1945*. Los Alamos, NM: Los Alamos Historical Society, 1999. 61. Print.

3. Los Alamos National Security. "The Debate." LANL.gov. *Los Alamos National Security*. 2009. Web. 20 Dec. 2009

4. Jennet Conant. *109 East Palace: Robert Oppenheimer and the Secret City of Los Alamos*. New York: Simon & Schuster, 2005. 386. Print.

5. Cynthia C. Kelly, *ed. The Manhattan Project: The Birth of the Atomic Bomb in the Words of Its Creators, Eyewitnesses, and Historians*. New York: Black Dog & Leventhal, 2007. xiv. Print.

6. Richard Rhodes. *The Making of the Atomic Bomb*. New York: Simon & Schuster, 1986. 751. Print.

INDEX

ABOUT THE AUTHOR

Sue Vander Hook has been writing and editing books for nearly 20 years. Her writing career began with several nonfiction books for adults and then focused on educational books for children and young adults. She especially enjoys writing about historical events and biographies of people who made a difference. Her published works also include a high school curriculum and series on disease, technology, and sports. Sue lives with her family in Mankato, Minnesota.

PHOTO CREDITS

AP Images, cover, 3, 11, 13, 19, 23, 25, 26, 37, 48, 58, 71, 75, 76, 82, 85, 86, 92, 95, 96, 97 (top), 97 (bottom), 98, 99 (top), 99 (bottom); S. Greg Panosian/iStockphoto, 6; John Verner/iStockphoto, 14; SSPL/Getty Images, 29; Los Alamos Historical Society, 33, 38, 47, 53, 57; Red Line Editorial, Inc., 42, 65, 66